LIGHT IS THE THEME:
LOUIS I. KAHN AND THE
KIMBELL ART MUSEUM

Comments on Architecture by Louis Kahn

Compiled by Nell E. Johnson

Kimbell Art Foundation, Fort Worth, Texas   1975

Kimbell Art Museum

3333 Camp Bowie Boulevard

Fort Worth, Texas 76107

First edition published 1975. Second printing 1978. Third printing 1988,
    with minor revisions and updated bibliography. Fourth printing 1994.

Fifth printing, revised and updated, 2002

Published in the United States of America

Library of Congress Catalog Card Number: 78-61163

International Standard Book Number: 0-912804-39-4

After the design of William D. Witliff, Encino Press, Austin, Texas

FOREWORD
TO THE THIRTIETH-ANNIVERSARY REPRINT

Light is the Theme was first published in 1975 to celebrate the achievement of Louis Kahn and all who had been involved in creating the Kimbell Art Museum. Thirty years on from the Museum's opening in 1972, we can now take the full measure of how great that achievement indeed was. During that time, the Kimbell has come to be recognized by architects and museum devotees around the world not only as Kahn's crowning masterpiece—the fullest and most perfect expression of his brilliant sensitivity to form, material, and light—but also as one of the finest museum buildings of the twentieth century. What Kahn, together with founding director Richard F. Brown and the board of the Kimbell Art Foundation created, was not just a beautiful work of architecture, but a vehicle that carries visitors along, structuring and modulating the experience they have of the Kimbell's collections. Sadly, Kahn was not fully able to appreciate how extraordinary those collections would be, as his untimely death in 1974 prevented him from seeing many of the famous masterpieces we now enjoy.

This reprint of Light is the Theme has been issued to coincide with the commemoration of the Kimbell's thirtieth anniversary in October 2002. It is a testament to Louis Kahn, Richard Brown, and all the others who made the Kimbell that the building and the art within it still speak to each other so eloquently. The famous "magic" of the Kimbell is as deserving of celebration today as when it first opened its doors.

Timothy Potts
Director
May 2002

INTRODUCTION

Concrete workers, carpenters, trustees, engineers, draftsmen, foremen, curators, and contractors—all these, and many more, were needed to build the Kimbell Art Museum. In the making of it we all had one of the grand privileges and opportunities of our lives, for it was not simply making, it was creating. The difference was there because the architect, Louis Kahn, was a great artist. In the beginning, the chasm between his protean vision and prosaic practicality, between idea and embodiment, sometimes seemed unbridgeable. But in the end everyone's comprehension of art's power to enlarge the dimensions of life was increased by helping to realize Lou Kahn's dream.

This book is intended to be more than the visual record of a building, more than a memorial to a beloved man. It is meant as an offering of thanks for his leading us, through his character and his art, to a fuller appreciation of why life is worth living.

All the pictures are of what Lou designed for us. The text consists solely of what he said. Identification of sources for both are given in an index and credit lines at the back of the book. One will also find there a page of basic facts about the building, as well as a listing of those people who contributed significantly to its success.

Richard F. Brown
Director, 1966–79

LOUIS ISIDORE KAHN

February 20, 1901–March 17, 1974

10

Silence to Light
Light to Silence
The threshold of their crossing
    is the Singularity
    is Inspiration
(Where the desire to express meets the possible)
    is the Sanctuary of Art
    is the Treasury of the Shadows
(Material casts shadows shadows belong to light)

A great American poet once asked the architect, 'What slice of the sun does your building have? What light enters your room?'—as if to say the sun never knew how great it is until it struck the side of a building.

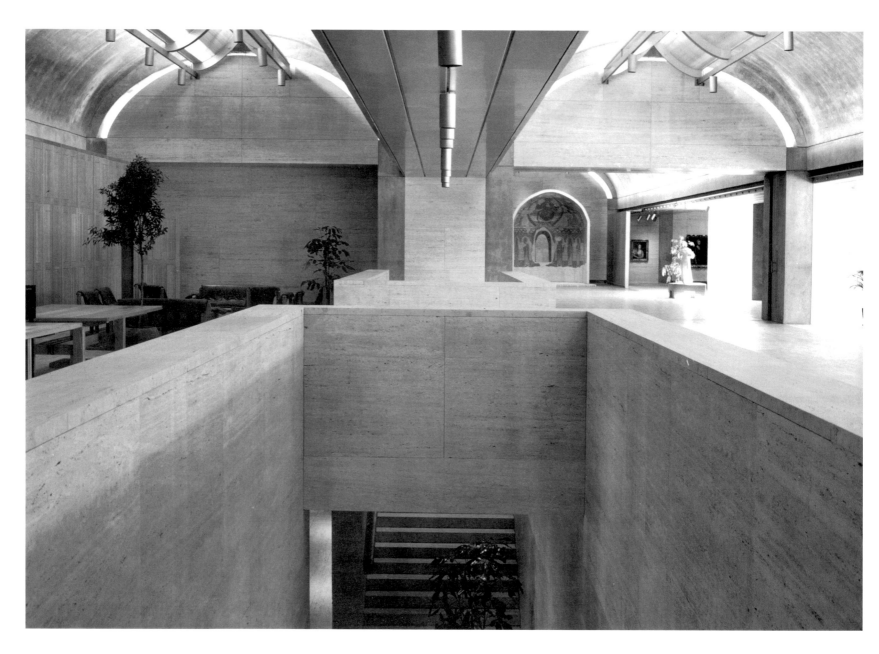

No space, architecturally, is a space unless it has natural light. . . . I am designing an art museum in Texas. Here I felt that the light in the rooms structured in concrete will have the luminosity of silver. I know that rooms for the paintings and objects that fade should only most modestly be given natural light. The scheme of enclosure of the museum is a succession of cycloid vaults each of a single span [100] feet long and [23] feet wide, each forming the rooms with a narrow slit to the sky, with a mirrored shape to spread natural light on the side of the vault. This light will give a glow of silver to the room without touching the objects directly, yet give the comforting feeling of knowing the time of day.

We knew that the museum would always be full of surprises. The blues would be one thing one day; the blues would be another thing another day, depending on the character of the light. Nothing static, nothing static as an electric bulb, which can only give you one iota of the character of light. So the museum has as many moods as there are moments in time, and never as long as the museum remains as a building will there be a single day like the other.

So this is a kind of invention that comes out of the desire to have natural light. Because it is the light the painter used to paint his painting. And artificial light is a static light . . . where natural light is a light of mood. And sometimes the room gets dark—why not?—and sometimes you must get close to look at it, and come another day, you see, to see it in another mood—a different time . . . to see the mood natural light gives, or the seasons of the year, which have other moods.

And the painting must reveal itself in different aspects if the moods of light are included in its viewing, in its seeing. This is another example of what one sets in his mind as being a nature of something. I think that's the nature, really, of a place where you see paintings. And research would never have given it to me because all I could find were ways of doing it completely contrary to the ways I think a museum might be. So it must be derived out of your own sense of its nature, of its service, of the nature of . . . the rooms of a museum.

And the cloud that passes over gives the room a feeling of association with the person that is in it, knowing that there is life outside of the room, and it reflects the life-giving that a painting does because I think a work of art is a giver of life. So light, this great maker of presences, can never be . . . brought forth by the single moment in light which the electric bulb has. And natural light has all the moods of the time of the day, the seasons of the year, [which] year for year and day for day are different from the day preceding.

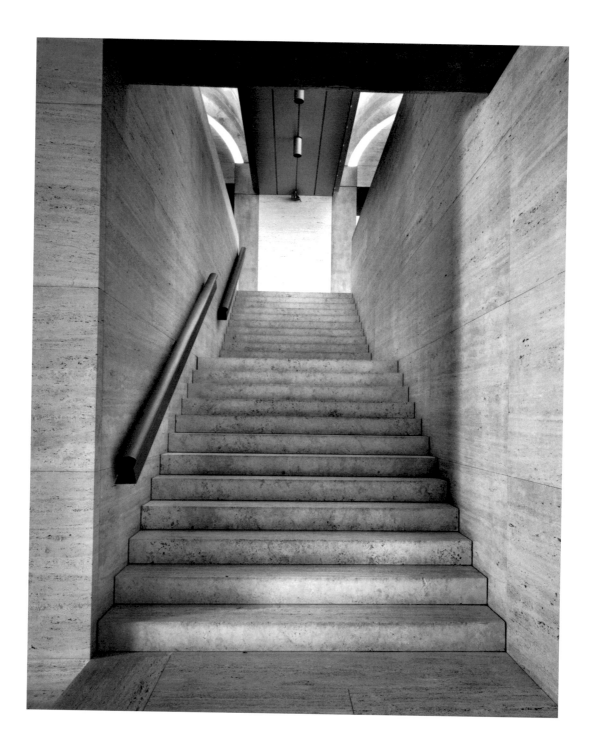

Structure is the giver of light.

A stair isn't something you get out of a catalogue but a very important event in a building.

Added to the skylight from the slit over the exhibit rooms, I cut across the vaults, at a right angle, a counterpoint of courts, open to the sky, of calculated dimensions and character, marking them Green Court, Yellow Court, Blue Court, named for the kind of light that I anticipate their proportions, their foliation, or their sky reflections on surfaces, or on water will give.

23

Of course there are some spaces which should be flexible, but there are also some which should be completely inflexible. They should be just sheer inspiration . . . just the place to *be*, the place which does not change, except for the people who go in and out.

Because of the open porches, how the building is made is completely clear before you go into it. It is the same realization behind Renaissance buildings, which gave the arcade to the street, though the buildings themselves did not need the arcade for their own purposes. So the porch sits there, made as the interior is made, without any obligation of paintings on its walls, a realization of what is architecture. When you look at the building and porch, it is as an offering. You know it wasn't programmed; it is something that emerged.

You know what's so wonderful about those porches? They're so unnecessary.

29

31

My mind is full of Roman greatness and the vault so etched itself in my mind that, though I cannot employ it, it's there always ready. And the vault seems to be the best. And I realize that the light must come from a high point where the light is best in its zenith. The vault, rising not high, not in an august manner, but somehow appropriate to the size of the individual. And its feeling of being home and safe came to mind.

By the nature of the vault-like structure, you have the play of lofty rooms with a space between each vault which has a ceiling at the level of the spring of the vault. The lower space does not have natural light, but gets it from the larger chamber. In the loftier rooms, how the room is made is manifest; the dimension of its light from above is manifest without partitions because the vaults defy division. Even when partitioned, the room remains a room. You might say that the nature of a room is that it always has the character of completeness.

This "natural lighting fixture" . . . is rather a new way of calling something; it is rather a new word entirely. It is actually a modifier of the light, sufficiently so that the injurious effects of the light are controlled to whatever degree of control is now possible. And when I look at it, I really feel it is a tremendous thing.

When a man says that he believes that natural light is something we are born out of, he cannot accept a school which has no natural light. He cannot even accept a movie house, you might say, which must be in darkness, without sensing that there must be a crack somewhere in the construction which allows enough natural light to come in to tell how dark it is. Now he may not demand it actually, but he demands it in his mind to be that important.

I put the glass between the structure members and the members which are not of structure because the joint is the beginning of ornament. And that must be distinguished from decoration which is simply applied. Ornament is the adoration of the joint.

Concrete does the work of structure, of holding things up. The columns are apart from each other. The space between must be filled. Therefore, the travertine. The travertine is a fill-in material. It is a wall material which is an enclosing material. . . . Travertine and concrete belong beautifully together because concrete must be taken for whatever irregularities or accidents in the pouring reveal themselves. Travertine is very much like concrete—its character is such that they look like the same material. That makes the whole building again monolithic and it doesn't separate things.

45

I don't like to see space nailed down. If you could move it and change it every day, fine.

auditorium, refreshment area
north court, galleries, portico

library, bookstore, lobby,
portico

galleries, conservator's court,
fountain court, portico

N ←   0 5   20   40 F
           2   5   10 M

shipping and receiving, shops   east entrance lobby, mechanical   offices, laboratories

N ←

0   5   20   40 F

2   5   10 M

CLIENT: Well, now that we have the general form, we have to put in all the guts and see if we can fit them in.

KAHN: If they don't all fit in easily and properly, then we have the wrong form.

Engineering is not one thing and design another. They must be one and the same thing.

51

When you have all the answers about a building before you start building it, your answers are not true. The building gives you answers as it grows and becomes itself.

Listen to the man who works with his hands. He may be able to show you a better way to do it.

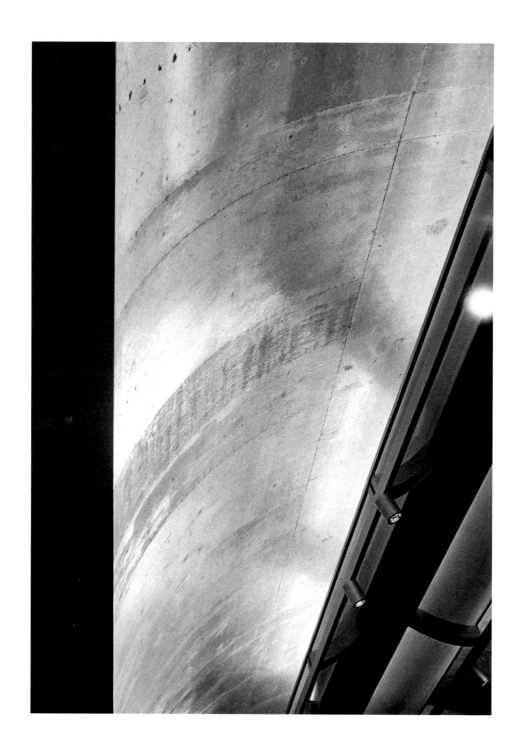

It is much better not to cover anything up but to show the full nature and relationship of part to part, including the present condition of each which is a record of how it got that way.

The world cannot be expected to come from the exercise of present technology alone to find the realms of new expression. I believe that technology should be inspired. A good plan demands it.

WILL ROGERS WEST

EXISTING AND NEW TREES

Mrs Kimbell – I hope
this sketch will help you
visualize at least the
main elements of the
Garden setting of the
K.A.M. –

LAWN

EXISTING TREES

EXISTING TREES

← VACATED WILL ROGERS EAST

LANCASTER

CAMP BOWIE BOULEVARD

ENTRANCE OF THE TREES

THE ENTRANCE TERRACE FORECOURT

Trough   fall of water   Trees   fall of water

walls & setting

PEDESTRIAN
ENTRANCE →

Steps   POOL

PORTICO.   PORTICO.

PEDESTRIAN
ENTRANCE ←

SOUTH
LOWER STEPPED
GARDEN
(GRASS THEATRE)

NORTH
P

TRUCK
LOWER
SERVICE
COURT
PARKING

NEW TREES

KIMBELL ART MUSEUM

↑

PARKING   PARKING

NEW TREES

AUTOMOBILE ENTRANCE   →

ARCH ADAMS STREET

SOUTH →

NORTH →

63

Dear Mrs Kimbell: Wednesday June 25 '69

I plan to come to see you soon to show and explain the garden ideas I have surrounding the Kimbell Art Museum. I hope you will find my work beautiful and meaningful.

The entrance of the trees is the entrance by foot which links Camp Bowie Boulevard and West Lancaster Ave. Two open porticos flank the entrance court of Terrace. In front of each portico is a reflecting pool which drops its water in a continuous sheet about 70 feet long in a basin two feet below. The sound would be gentle. The stepped entrance court passes between the porticos and their pools with a fountain, around which one sits, on axis designed to be the source of the portico pools. The west lawn gives the building perspective.

The south garden is at a level 10 feet below the garden entrance approached by gradual stepped lawns shaped to be a place to sit to watch the performance of a play music or dance the building with its arched silhouette acting as the back drop of a stage. When not so in use it will seem only as a garden where sculpture acquired from time to time would be.

The North Garden though mostly utilitarian is designed with ample trees to shield and balance the south and North sides of the building

The car entrance and parking is also at the lower level, running parallel to Arch Adams street. This end too is lined with trees designed to overhang the cars as shelter. For This we must choose the right tree whose habits are respectful to the car tops.

When I see you I expect to bring a model which should say more than my little words

By now you know that I cannot be present at the ground breaking ceremony. Unfortunately I have emergency duties in India at the same Time. In my absence I wish everything well.
I am confident that the work will progress well from now on. I believe every one believes in the building and its good purposes
I expect to return from India by the 12th of July. I will need a few weeks to firm up the material I hope to present to you for discussion.

Sincerely Yours
Louis I Kahn

SITE PLAN

0 5   20   40 F
2   5   10 M

→ N

66

I don't believe in need as a force at all. Need is a current, everyday affair. But desire—that is something else again. Desire is the forerunner of a new need. It is the yet not stated, the yet not made which motivates.

A module is not the repetition of a motif but the expression of an architectural principle.

This building feels—and it's a good feeling—that I had nothing to do with it, that some other hand did it.

ARCHITECT

Louis I. Kahn, FAIA, architect
Project architect: Marshall D. Meyers
Associate architect: Preston M. Geren and Associates
Project coordinator: Frank H. Sherwood

CONSULTANTS

Structure: August E. Komendant
Lighting: Richard Kelly; Edison Price
Acoustics: C. P. Boner and Associates
Landscape: George Patton
Graphics and exhibition design: Laurence Channing
Electronics: Thomas Electronics

CONSTRUCTION

General contractor: Thos. S. Byrne, Inc.
Project manager: A. T. Seymour, III
Job supervisor: Virgil Earp
Landscape: Vernon S. Swanson

CLIENT

Kimbell Art Foundation
Museum director: Richard F. Brown
On-site representative: E. B. Brown

CHRONOLOGY

April 13, 1964	Death of Kay Kimbell
November 9, 1964	Announcement of Museum and site by the Kimbell Art Foundation and the city of Fort Worth
September 28, 1965	Appointment of Museum director, Richard F. Brown
October 6, 1966	Architectural contract let
May 5, 1969	General construction contract let
June 29, 1969	Groundbreaking ceremony
August 3, 1972	Completion of Museum building
October 4, 1972	Opening of Museum

AWARDS

1972	Best Building Award, National General Contractors Association
1973	Lumen Award, Illuminating Engineers Society
1975	Honor Award and Bartlett Award, American Institute of Architects
1975	Engineering Excellence Award, Consulting Engineers Council of Texas, Inc.
1982	Award of Excellence, The Art Museum Association
1983	Citation of Honor, Texas Society of Architects
1997	Twenty-Five Year Award, Texas Society of Architects
1998	Twenty-Five Year Award, American Institute of Architects
1998	Twenty-Five Year Award, Fort Worth Chapter, American Institute of Architects

SITE

The museum is situated on nine and one-half acres in Amon Carter Square Park, a cultural complex including the Amon Carter Museum, the Modern Art Museum of Fort Worth, the William Edrington Scott Theater, the Fort Worth Museum of Science and History, the Will Rogers Memorial Coliseum and Auditorium, and the Casa Manaña Theater.

ORGANIZATION

Sixteen narrow rectangular vaulted elements are laid out in three sections with six vaults side by side on each end and four in the middle; flat-roofed inverted channels separate the vaults. Two elements are eliminated in the center of the west side to make an entrance court. The sloping site gives public access from this court to the upper (gallery) level. Lower-level access is from parking lots on the north and east sides. The vaulted roofs articulate specific areas on the gallery level while interior courtyards punctuate the flow of open space. The east entrance lobby separates the sections on each end, which house administrative and shop areas. Mechanical and electrical distribution systems are contained in a full basement.

STRUCTURE

Vaults are roofed by 24-by-104-foot clear-span cycloid shells of post-tensioned reinforced concrete. Each is supported on four 2-by-2-foot corner columns. Vaults covering interior spaces measure 20 by 100 feet and have a longitudinal $2\frac{1}{2}$-foot slit at the apex with concrete cross struts every 10 feet. Lower edges of the shells support 7-foot reinforced concrete channels with aluminum soffits that house the air and electrical distribution systems. Exterior travertine infill walls have a reinforced concrete core between columns. Two-way post-tensioning is used in upper-level floor slabs. The lower level is conventional poured-in-place concrete of pan-formed slab and joist construction.

MATERIALS

Exterior: Poured-in-place concrete with as-cast surface is used for the structure. Diamond-sawn, unfilled travertine veneer from Bagni di Tivoli, Italy, is used for infill walls, court paving, steps, and wall copings. Lead-coated copper roofs the shells. The public parking area is of dark brown square brick pavers. Cedar brown marble aggregate is used for the staff parking lot, walkways, and pool bottoms. Loose chips of the marble cover the entrance court beneath the rows of yaupon holly trees. Curbs and pool linings are of Andes black granite. Double insulating glass is used on the gallery level; polycarbonate and acrylic sheeting covers the light slits. Doors and frames, windows and bollards are of mill-finish stainless steel.

Interior: The same as-cast concrete is used for the structure, and travertine for infill walls, stairs, balustrade and portions of floors. Remaining gallery flooring, doors, frames, and cabinetwork are of quarter-sawn white oak. Slate flooring is used in the kitchen. Soffits and reflectors are made of anodized aluminum. Mill-finish stainless steel is used for elevators and kitchen, with blasted mill-finish stainless steel for handrails.

DIMENSIONS

Gross area is 120,000 square feet (11,150²) with galleries approximately 22,000 square feet. Overall length (north-south) is 318 feet. Width at the widest roofed area is 174 feet and at the narrow center section, 114 feet. Height to the apex of a vault from the floor is 20 feet, and overall building height from the lowest (east) ground level is 40 feet.

COST

Construction: $6.5 million
Original equipment and furniture: $1 million

INDEX

33   Interview with Patsy Swank for KERA-TV, Dallas, October 27, 1973.

34   "Kimbell Art Museum, Fort Worth," *The Architectural Forum*, vol. 137, no. 1 (July–August 1972): 59.

35   South exhibition galleries (facing north)

36   Detail of the pierced aluminum reflector

37, 38   Interview with Marshall D. Meyers, Philadelphia, August 11, 1972.

39   Louis Kahn in the auditorium

40   Cabinetwork: doors leading from the east lobby to the shop area

41   Detail of concrete wall showing imprint of formwork and lead plugs in form-tie holes

42   East exterior showing 3-foot separation between sections

43   Interview with Patsy Swank for KERA-TV, Dallas, October 27, 1973.

44   Interview with Marshall D. Meyers, Philadelphia, August 11, 1972.

45   West exterior, detail of portico

46   North exhibition galleries

47   Conversation with the client, October 1966.

48, 49   Upper (gallery level) floor plan (roofing system indicated by dotted lines); lower (service) level floor plan. On both plans a solid line indicates structural elements, a hatched line infill material.

50   Discussion between client and architect, 1968.

51   Glass-walled carpenter's shop

52   Construction procedure, January 18, 1971. Flat slab units were poured first to provide working platforms. Vaults were poured on top of hinged breakaway forms seen both lowered and raised, covered and with ribs yet exposed. On the south end, left, four short completed vaults are seen ready for insulation; the center vault is insulated, papered, and ready for the final sheath of lead roofing.

53   Conversation with the client, 1971.

54   Conversation with the client, 1971. Virgil Earp, job supervisor, contributed significantly in developing the technology necessary to get the shells built.

55   Pouring a cycloid vault, January 26, 1972. Over the smooth-coated underlying forms a 4-inch-thick shell of reinforced concrete was poured and braced with post-tensioning cables (not visible under the 2-by-6-inch blockers).

56   Pouring the library mezzanine floor, June 23, 1971. With slight differences, the library mezzanine floor resembles the gallery level floor, utilizing two-way post-tensioning and styrofoam blocks to lighten the load of the solid cast slab.

CREDITS

Photography: Michael Bodycomb: 10; Robert Wharton: 13, 19, 20, 24, 30, 39, 51, 52, 55, 56, 58, 62, 67, 68, 71; Marshall D. Meyers: 14, 25, 26, 41, 42, 46, 57, 61; Geoff Winningham: 29, 35, 40, 45; Robert Shaw: cover, 23, 36; Ezra Stoller: 72; B. V. Doshi, 9.

Plans: Anna Ku

SELECTED BIBLIOGRAPHY

These references are in addition to sources cited in the index. For discussions of the architectural program, the evolution of design, and illustrations of early sketches and models, see: Peter Plagens, "Louis Kahn's New Museum in Fort Worth," *Artforum* 6 (February 1968): 18–23; "Kahn's Museum: An Interview with Richard F. Brown," *Art in America* 60 (September–October 1972): 44–48; *Louis I. Kahn: Sketches for the Kimbell Art Museum*, exhibition organized by David M. Robb Jr., with essay by Marshall D. Meyers (Fort Worth, 1978); Heinz Ronner and Sharad Jhaveri, *Louis I. Kahn: Complete Work, 1935–1974*, 2nd rev. and enlarged ed. (Basel and Boston: 1987), 340–47; *The Louis I. Kahn Archive: Personal Drawings*, vol. 5 (New York and London, 1989), 194–287; *In Pursuit of Quality: The Kimbell Art Museum, An Illustrated History of the Art and Architecture*, with essay by Patricia Cummings Loud (Fort Worth, 1987), 9–95; Patricia Cummings Loud, *The Art Museums of Louis I. Kahn* (Durham and London, 1989), 100–171.

Structural design, engineering, and construction are discussed in: A. T. Seymour III, "Post-tensioned Shells Form Museum Roof," *Engineering News-Record* 187 (November 11, 1971): 24–25; A. T. Seymour III, "Contractor Challenged by Kimbell Art Museum Design," *Texas Contractor* (November 1972); A. T. Seymour III, "The Immeasurable Made Measurable: Building the Kimbell Art Museum," *Via* 7 (1984): 75–85; August E. Komendant, *Contemporary Concrete Structures* (New York, 1972), 504–8; Komendant, *18 Years with Architect Louis I. Kahn* (Englewood, N.J., 1975), 115–31; Guy Nordenson, "The Lineage of Structure and the Kimbell Art Museum," *Lotus International* 98 (1998): 24–48; *Louis I. Kahn: The Construction of the Kimbell Art Museum*, ed. Luca Bellinelli, rev. ed., with essays by Joseph Rykwert, Patricia Cummings Loud, Marshall D. Meyers, and Aurelio Muttoni (Milan, 1999).

Architectural assessments and comprehensive illustrations are presented in: Richard Kelly, "Lighting Starts with Daylight," *Progressive Architecture* 54 (September 1973): 82–85; William H. Jordy, "The Span of Kahn," *Architectural Review* 155 (June 1974): 318–42; Andrea O. Dean, "Honor Awards Go to Nine Buildings," *AIA Journal* 63 (May 1975): 26–43; "Louis I. Kahn," with essay by Famihiko Maki, *Architecture and Urbanism* (1975): 53–72, 315–21; Meyers, *Louis I. Kahn: Yale University Art Gallery, New Haven, Connecticut, 1951–53; Kimbell Art Museum, Fort Worth, Texas, 1966–72*, ed. Yukio Futagawa, *Global Architecture* 38 (Tokyo, 1976); Meyers, "Masters of Light: Louis Kahn," *AIA Journal* 68 (September 1979): 100–107; John Lobell, *Between Silence and Light: Spirit in the Architecture of Louis I. Kahn* (Boulder, 1979), 39 (illus.), 94–99; Thomas Hoving, "A Gem of a Museum," *Connoisseur* 210 (May 1982): 86–95; Lawrence W. Speck, "Evaluation: The Kimbell Art Museum," *AIA Journal* 71 (August 1982): 36–43; "Louis I. Kahn," *Architecture and Urbanism* (special ed., 1983): 128–57, 196, 198, 223–27; Alexandra Tyng, *Beginnings: Louis I. Kahn's Philosophy of Architecture* (New York, 1984): 53–55, 150–55, 170, 175; *Louis I. Kahn, l'uomo, il maestro*, ed. and trans. Alessandra Latour (Rome, 1986); Richard Saul Wurman, *What Will Be Has Always Been: The Words of Louis I. Kahn* (New York, 1986), 159, 177, 235–42, 216; "After Architecture: The Kimbell Art Museum," ed. Richard Ingersoll, essays by Doug Suisman, Dana Cuff, Peter McCleary, P. Loud, *Design Book Review* 11 (Winter 1987): 35–55; Roger Kimball, "How to Build a Museum: the Example of Louis Kahn," *The New Criterion* 8, no. 10 (June 1990): 64–67; Michael Benedikt, *Deconstructing the Kimbell* (New York, 1991); David B. Brownlee and David G. De Long, *Louis I. Kahn: In the Realm of Architecture,* with essay by P. Loud (Los Angeles and New York, 1991), 130–33, 266–87, 396–99; Vincent Scully, "Louis I. Kahn and the Ruins of Rome," *MoMA* 12 (1991): 12; Brendan Gill, "Primary Elements," *New Yorker* (February 15, 1992): 84; Michael Brawn, *The Kimbell Art Museum: Louis I. Kahn* (London, 1992); Martin Filler, "America's Best Architect," *The New York Review of Books* 40 (February 11, 1993): 16–20; Martin Filler, "The Emperor of Light: Kahn's Oeuvre, Twenty Years Later," *Monografías de Arquitectura y Vivienda* 44 (Nov.–Dec. 1993): 22–30, 80–87, 104–07; Kenneth Frampton, *Studies in Tectonic Culture* (Cambridge, 1995): 239–46.